History Of Japan For Kids

A History Series

Children Explore Histories Of The World Edition

SPEEDY
PUBLISHING

Speedy Publishing LLC
40 E. Main St. #1156
Newark, DE 19711
www.speedypublishing.com

Few nations on Earth have had a more colorful history than Japan. Read and learn more of Japan's rich history!

Japan likely was settled about 35,000 years ago by Paleolithic people from the Asian mainland.

At the end of
the last Ice Age,
about 10,000
years ago, a
culture called
the Jomon
developed.
Jomon hunter-
gatherers
fashioned
fur clothing,
wooden houses,
and elaborate
clay vessels.

A second wave of settlement around 400 B.C. by the Yayoi people introduced metal-working, rice cultivation, and weaving to Japan.

The first era of recorded history in Japan is the Kofun (250-538 A.D.), characterized by large burial mounds or tumuli.

Buddhism came to Japan during the Asuka Period, 538-710, as did the Chinese writing system.

Japan's unique culture developed rapidly in the Heian era, 794-1185, the samurai warrior class developed at this time.

Samurai lords, called "shoguns," took over governmental power in 1185, and ruled Japan in the name of the emperor until 1868.

A strong emperor, Go-Daigo, tried to overthrew shogunal rule in 1331, resulting in a civil war between competing northern and southern courts that finally ended in 1392.

In that
year, a new
constitutional
monarchy was
established,
headed by the
Meiji Emperor.
The power of
the shoguns
was broken.

After the Meiji Emperor's death, his son became the Taisho Emperor (r. 1912-1926).

Japan formalized its rule over Korea and seized northern China during World War I.

The Showa
Emperor, Hirohito, (r.
1926-1989) oversaw
Japan's aggressive
expansion during
World War II, its
surrender, and its
rebirth as a modern,
industrialized
nation.

The Four-Tiered Class System of Feudal Japan

The Samurai Class

The Farmers/ Peasants

The Artisans

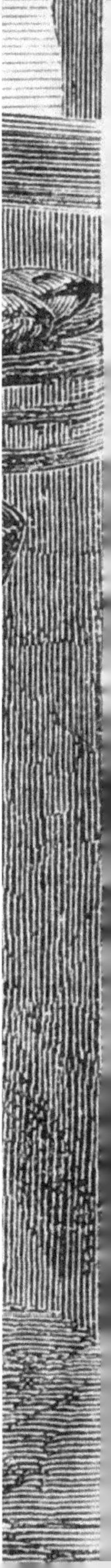

The Merchants

The **Japanese History** is very interesting, research and learn more!